Plucking the Stinger

STEPHANIE ROGERS

saturnalia books

Distributed by University Press of New England
Hanover and London

Saturnalia Books
105 Woodside Rd.
Ardmore, PA 19003
info@saturnaliabooks.com

ISBN: 978-0-9962206-8-2
Library of Congress Control Number: 2016944134

Book Design by Saturnalia Books
Printing by McNaughton & Gunn
Cover Art: "The Nursery" by Regan Rosburg, original artwork.

Distributed by:
University Press of New England
1 Court Street
Lebanon, NH 03766
800-421-1561

Grateful acknowledgment is made to the editors of the following publications in which several poems in this collection have previously appeared, sometimes in slightly different form:

Another Chicago Magazine: "Operations on My Other, Lesser Self"; *Best New Poets 2013*: "How It Kept On"; *Cincinnati Review*: "Ode to My Despair"; *Cream City Review*: "Another Way the Body Dies," "The Incident When My Dog Dies and/or You Leave Me"; *Grist: A Journal for Writers*: "My Despair Airs Her Grievances"; *HIV Here & Now Anthology*: "HIV Test Results: False Positive"; *The Journal*: "Mental Hospital," "Running Out of Medication"; *Linebreak*: "Naming Goodbye"; *Louisville Review*: "No Return Address"; *Madison Review*: "My Year in the Bootleg Porn Industry"; *Mid-American Review*: "Story"; *New Ohio Review*: "Phone Call," "We Remember You for Now"; *The Pinch*: "Half Perfume, Half Something Rotten"; *Pleiades*: "Beating the Shit Out of My Despair"; *Ploughshares*: "So Long"; *Southern Review*: "Dear Sophia," "On the Occasion of Her Annual Disappointment"; *Spoon River Poetry Review*: "Symphony for Red"; *Third Coast*: "Elegy"; *upstreet*: "What Happened," "Sleeping with Sonny Ghosthorse"; *Wisconsin Review*: "Serving Ice Cream to Joaquin Phoenix."

"Symphony for Red" was reprinted in *Best New Poets 2006*. "On the Occasion of Her Annual Disappointment" was reprinted in *Best New Poets 2009*.

Thank you to all my teachers at The Ohio State University, the University of Cincinnati, the University of North Carolina at Greensboro, Brooklyn Poets, and the 24PearlStreet Online Writing Program, especially Andrew Hudgins, Kathy Fagan, Joanie Mackowski, John Drury, Don Bogen, Stuart Dischell, Linda Gregg, Jessica Greenbaum, and Ada Limón.

I would also like to thank Sophia Kartsonis, Amber Leab, Daniel Kaczmarek, Kia Westwood, Christina Duhig, Lauren Moseley, Sarah Rose Nordgren, and especially Kerri French, for their careful reading of this book before it was a book.

My deepest gratitude to Henry Israeli at Saturnalia Books for giving this book a home, to Christopher Salerno for the thoughtful edits, and to Regan Rosburg for the beautiful cover art.

Thanks to the following people for their encouragement over the years and for believing in my work: Todd Doyle, Natalie Holland, Matthew Feltman, Josh Bell, Christopher Culwell, Leigh Kolb, and Joseph Gartrell (for tallying the wins).

So much gratitude to Jessica Greenbaum, Ada Limón, and Cate Marvin for their kind and generous words; to Maria Deutscher and John Morrow, for pulling me out of my own head; and to Josh Ralske, who found me.

Most of all, thank you to my parents, without whom I wouldn't have written a word of this, and thanks to my sister, Heather, and my brother, Ian, who sustain me despite everything.

The poem, "What Happened," borrows a line from Ann Lauterbach's poem, "Hum," and "Half Perfume, Half Something Rotten" takes its title from the Stephen Dunn poem, "Privilege." "Dear Sophia" is for Sophia Kartsonis. Many of the poems in the third section of this book are in memory of Joel McKanna and are dedicated to Heather McKanna.

Table of Contents

For Sophia, Chloe, and Penelope

1. Pluck: To Play Gently

ON THE OCCASION OF HER ANNUAL DISAPPOINTMENT

I woke in the night, and begonias flew from my mouth.
Happy Birthday: this could be a long one. You can imagine

the lump, fist-sized, throbbing in the throat from those
unraveling bulbs. Then, the girl who looks like me, talks

like me, lives straight and thoroughly out of laundry baskets
like me, she almost wept. Well, actually. I woke weird,

hand fat with sleep. The girl in my mirror shook, curled up
at the bottom, scratched the glass so hard a fingernail flew.

When I opened my mouth to calm her, *there there*,
the flowers gathered like ulcers, shot up from my stomach,

the long stem of the esophagus, then bloomed angrily
at the voice box. Begonias. And the girl who appears

in my mirror every birthday to carve her little celebration—
another year down, and we're still here—screamed, delighted.

Okay, truthfully. I woke bleeding at the mouth, grinding
teeth. My tongue: stabbed by an incisor. Droplets bloomed

on the lower lip, like the residue of wine. Sometimes,
I pour a bottle for the girl in me, when it's her birthday,

and no one has given her flowers.

OPERATIONS ON MY OTHER, LESSER SELF

Hello in there, ruined and inappropriate heart.
I've come bearing a toothbrush and a reason
not to return the surgical scissors, the joint, art
books, the spit-shined shoes, aim, everything.

I've come bearing a tooth, a brush, and a reason
for cradling your bird-egg cheek, for shredding
books, the spit, shined shoes, aim, everything
with a god or fingertips. When the sun's red,

cradling a bird egg against her cheek, shredding
the day, I walk the hilltop with a stethoscope
and God. My fingertips listen to your sun-red
face like ten cast-off bones digging a scalpel

into the day. I walk the hilltop as a stethoscope
aiming to hear everything caged, everything's
tin face, bones cast off by my digging scalpel.
Hello, I said, I never wanted this endlessness,

aiming to hear everything. Caged, everything's
lonely, baring teeth, and like you, repeating
a hello I said I never wanted. That endlessness
thuds like a dirty shovel on a coffin, remember?

I'm lonely, baring teeth, and like you, repeating
my mistakes undercover, so only the eager hear
the shoveled dirt thudding the coffin. Remember,
I brought a reason to find you, brushes to clean

you, to uncover you here in my eager mistakes.
I'm haunted by what nests in you, what hole
I brought, brushing to find you a clean reason
to love. In the beginning, I saw, aimed to steal

what nests, what hole I'm haunted by. In you,
the stitches rip too often, fall out, don't take
to love in the beginning. I saw, aimed to steal
another. Who are we? Cut up inside again,

the stiches rip too often, fall out, or don't take
to surgery, the scissors I return for our joint art.
Who are we to cut up, our own insides again
ruined and inappropriate? Heart, hello in there?

BEATING THE SHIT OUT OF MY DESPAIR

*Look, it's not necessarily my fault you stopped taking
your meds, Bitch.* And then I punched her in the womb.
Whiskey. To think I used to call her the Kamikaze

Kisser. On the night in question, I swallowed her
tongue stud. The x-ray showed, days later, the piercing
had left the building. Until then, her body had not yet

occurred to me, though she rolled down a hill once
on a suicide mission. Bees. Over the course
of the night in question: gestures. What they meant was

*if we don't particularly like each other, let's not
particularly pretend.* That shouldn't have been so hard
to say. If there was a moon, it dripped its conjured face

onto the landscape. And lo! It did cast a heavy glow
upon the bubs! I mean bulbs. In the shadow, her hands
looked like an octopus. I was freezing my ass off.

The night in question had me saddled, throwing all
that stupid silence on the fire but screaming, *Don't cross
the line, seismic longing, wearing that face.* She told me

I should be more careful who I align myself with,
and she said it right into the proverbial microphone.
Her voice sounded like that one time, testing

the reverb. She made so much sense I wore my hair down,
like a real girl. I told her, *There are differences between us,
Perky. You're admittedly quite the killjoy sprung*

from some unrequited heat. She answered how
the liars answer, hocking her grandmother's diamond
with one hand, writing everything down with the other.

ANOTHER WAY THE BODY DIES

Part of me thinks I shot someone
a few weeks ago, but who knows
if I know the difference between a gun fired
and a plucked weed. Eventually everything
I touch sprouts a gray vine and dies. My
eyes always find what's rotting around the room,
but I don't say a word. Now I listen,
while rain drums fuck you fuck you and you.

All month it's been like this, the same lull,
and me in bed outlining the tears
on the wall where paint dripped dry.
I used to have a face made of glass, and all
my friends looked away, afraid to ask for what
they wanted. The days dissolved
like a wet pill back then. Back then, I slept
with a bullet under my tongue.

I LIKE WATCHING THE GURNEY WHEELED INTO THE HUSH

I like the baseball cap propped on the park bench,
the dog owner's peeking crimson thong.
I like the makeshift noose
in that cloudbank, the organ playing
in the background of a scream. My childhood
invention of the rooftop woman. And to bang the soft
part of my palms together but still make a sound
no louder than the blue
bass line pumping down a thigh.
I like to aggravate the eardrum with a record scratch.
And not only in darkness. I like the parasite
that crawls into the gills
of fish, devouring the tongue, becoming it.
Who hasn't wanted to take up residence in a mouth?

SERVING ICE CREAM TO JOAQUIN PHOENIX

I expected to make a cone
with something flavored cherry.
Instead, he ordered chocolate in a cup.
I said, "Joaquin, I think
you'd really like the Cherry Cordial," and his lips
formed a tender smirk, baiting me.

"Here's a cup of Cherry Cordial, on me,"
I said. His eyes turned cone-
colored and smoky. I stared at the lip-
stick mark on his shirt collar, a cherry
print puckering, a blood stain. "I think
I asked for chocolate," he said, "in a cup

if you don't mind." I reached out to cup
his stubbled chin, but he stopped me,
held my hand. I couldn't think.
An ice cream crystal shivered down a cone.
A cherry fell. Why'd I offer Cherry
Cordial anyway—his mouth curling, lips

chewed up and tired? It must've been his lips,
pink and ice cream tinted, and the couple
just behind us, kissing, sharing cherries.
I said, "Sorry Joaquin. Leave it to me
to screw up a simple ice cream cone."
"A cup," he said. "No cone." I thought, "I think

he thinks me weird." I tried, "I think
I liked you best in *Quills*," then licked the lip
scar just below his nostril. A cone
crumbled down my hand. He handed me a cup.
Nothing moved. "Look at me,"
I said, as I moved from Cherry

Cordial to the chocolate bin. "I'm cherry-
flavored and lovely, don't you think?"
He said, "Believe me. Believe me,"
although I don't know what it meant. Lips
tell lies, and tongues curl up to cup
another's tongue. I scooped a chocolate cone.

"On me," I said, then topped it with a cherry.
Down the cone it fell. I think he smiled when he left—
his lips curled over the cup he stole—I couldn't tell.

MY YEAR IN THE BOOTLEG PORN INDUSTRY

All that's known of me is I'm some trouble,
a coughing house cat, and once recycled rain
pecking the bureau. So, watch out someone.
There's my new porno in the VCR, not wrong,
not right, but there. Some say you're a creep
for watching, Daniel, that ridiculous scene

where all the roads lead to that obscene
farmer, hacking on his death bed, trouble
with his greasy heart. Who wouldn't creep
away, clattering, while I pulled the reins
attached to a white trash neck? Wrongly,
I pushed a sex ring, though it was someone

else and his idea. See, he wanted some. One
time, for fun, I burned Joe's belt, and he'd seen
it all and made me brand the hard, wrong
side of the buckle someplace nasty. Trouble
with that boy. He rained like me, rained
like a waterfall with a clown face, a creepy

sudsing eye. Big world to love in, a crêpe,
fruit-filled, impossible not to miss someone
with this least suffering. Once I let one reign
long. His name was Leaf, a mostly unseen
pot-smoking someplace and all that rubble
piling up, up. Sister, everything was wrong

then, three-legged and missing teeth, wrong
like me posing on the nude piano in crepe,
too, and how I wore a railroad track, troubled
the photographer for mascara and someone
unshaven in a cop disguise. In that scene,
Frank pulled me from my drowning, drained

the bathtub before the hair clog won. Rain
now, and I still haven't made up the wrong
face for the moon, my best blush, ashen
eyes. Matthew, if this is love, I'm a creeper,
a candy bar on summer pavement, some un-
discovered beauty, dead. That's the trouble

with the underground porn scene, all that rain
transplanted, and the trouble with the wrong
men, a sum: one wide smile creeping a spoon.

MY DESPAIR AIRS HER GRIEVANCES

You've made a hobby of bringing out
our hideous self, boring self, our plant-watering self,

our wake up on time and eat a big bowl of Cheerios
self, our showering, enormous,

flossing self, because you're the kind of person who
pays close attention

to the indie film's dialogue, photographs
the spider webs, enjoys your daily morning

coffee and makes me eye-roll,
makes me Richard

Marx, makes me pasta and marinara, fat-free dressing,
side salad, makes me Desperate

Housewives, the ice cream truck jingle,
the Middletown Middies' fight song, the Friday night

marching band after-party
cookout at Mr. Hunt's, when damn you I want

zombie hookups, graveyard beer pong,
want pyrotechnic bedroom waterfalls, a 20 x 20 wall-

mounted Ouija board,
our defied-the-DSM psychosis,

a female foot fetish and our BDSM
dom-gear, Walmart layaway plan paid off, want a rush

hour Interstate performance of our childhood
complete with hooker lookalikes,

a crack pipe, silicone, syringes, but you'd rather have
the midday napping you, the pet-

sitting for a neighbor you,
the studio audience-prompted laughter you,

all ponytail, all yoga, all wrapping
Christmas presents you, even though she always floats

away, like a mosquito in a swamp storm, barely
visible, and craving blood.

FOR SAFETY REASONS, I'M MEDICATING
MY FREAK SHOW

Soon I'll miss my screw-
    Sleeked underbelly
Jack hammer. My come-
    wildly unsophisticated.
storm. Shunned by goddess
    dreams. Run-stung shins.
stick incongruous crotch
    My face pixilated. High
brassiere. My screaming
    My thyroid fishnets.
with the marshmallow splat.
    Face down acrobatic swish!
sprain from the one-
    thrust. Thirst. Can't-breathe
Un-psychotropic. Un-
    confusion. Non-containment.
the cafeteria trashcan.
    maker. Prison jacket
The forgotten time wart
    And I got ugly!
Got a melancholy halfwit
    in the heart wing! I'll miss
shut-up oboe ringtone
    lurk. Senseless shy boat
Oceanic undercut. And my
    My ripped skin smile.
and hangnail blood drink.
    Oh my salt-dissolved
placebo eyeball
    online plant killer. Miss
in the hollyhock field.

ball comedy hair song.
    of my spicy sun. Jack rabbit.
uppance, and my come
    Disgraced in the sand-
and god of the flapping
    I'll miss them too. Like a shit
and triangle freak tong.
    jinx of the stoned and horned
sore, bruise perfumed.
    Mustached campground
Face gone lovely!
    My globbed hand
armed hookup. I'll miss my
    diseased brain.
stabilized and paperclipped
    My retainer lost hopscotching
Cheese grater. Milkshake
    sodomy. Zit song sky bone.
risen from the ginseng.
    Got surrendered!
sugar lump bubbled
    the shake date. My sorry
voice and happy love
    radiating in the hail.
trademark breath mint.
    My chipped fingernail
Oh my napkin kite!
    throat gurgle! New
worsening! I'll miss you,
    you, cigarette bible
Miss shanghai pumpkin.

Miss dripping sweat
contraband fantastic.
            pump. My Mississippi
cock fucker. Uncle son
            my backward
pit! My alcohol

            bomb toke. My comb over
And my eyeliner vein
            hologram. Rabbit hole
of a shithead co-opting
            buggy. My blaring stomach
redacted!

ODE TO MY DESPAIR

O my despair, how dare you come to me, mornings
before I've even risen. I stare at you like a stain
on my mother's heirloom quilt. You, scuffed baby shoe

lying in the grocery store parking lot, black Velcro
in place of laces: let's walk together awhile. I want to
get to know you better, decapitated head of a dandelion,

the pigeon swarm, and the lost appointment book.
O my despair, how dare you come to me, all morning
light when I want the meteor shower. How you linger.

You give six-year-olds the finger. Wait, do I like you
a little, secretly, when you wean me from my exercise
routine, my washed and scented hair, my fresh-

cleaned jeans? Oh fuck off, ocean dragging me through
riptides, swollen eyeball scratched by a grandmother's
necklace during the hug. O my despair, how dare you

come to me, mourning the latest suicide: this time
with a syringe. Maybe stay for just a minute? Even
though you're playing hopscotch on my eardrum with

a needle, and you make my heart feel like a paper cutout
torn and pinned to a corkboard. I love you the way you
love me, freely, and in need. I hate you like an audience

at the ballet, interrupted by a DJ scratching records.
O my despair, how dare you come to me. I swallow
your gut punch and raise you a brim-filled glass of pills.

2. Pluck: To Pull Away Quickly

ELEGY

At some point, I got off track. But the moon kept churning out

that sky. Ask me my name. I'll tell you

about a boy in a Camaro, a boy in a pair of oil-stained

cargo pants, that boy dousing his life

with gasoline and a mean flame.

I used to love to take

an ice cube in my mouth, run it down his neck

until it vanished. You wouldn't believe

the skies then: midnight still

hanging onto daylight like the moon was a rag

dried stiff on a clothesline. Most of the time

I couldn't tell you

when night ended and morning took over,

when I first confused a boy in a graveyard

for a god removing

his wristwatch with his teeth. But there were days, too,

days when the sun awoke in a pick-up truck

filled with ash. And that sky looked like it might never recover.

MY DESPAIR DISCUSSES MY COMMITMENT ISSUES

You must be in a fight with your boyfriend. I know you
dangle the headphones in front of him like the music is
his one last chance. But he's suturing the fabric of your
favorite teddy. He's a riot and trying out the old brand
of escape. Prying open your closed mouth and moving

through it. Painting *you're dead* on the new man you're
screwing. You want to steal his eye? Then steal it. Don't
want to nurse him back? Then fake it. Honey, it's a long
nightmare, always playing it cool: not young enough to
shake it anymore, not old enough to up the ante, to take

the loss back, or scratch it off. My deranged voice yells
you're on fire! Yes, a mess ensues if you buy too much
time. Five minutes ago, you told your boyfriend *no one.*
Now you don't recall a thing. Teach me how to kill me,
and I'll kill me. Show me where I bit you, and I'll break

me. Tell me why you only love him to his face or where
the latest séance plays tonight. What will you resurrect
with all those missing teeth stored and ticking in your
wine glass? You must be in a fight with your boyfriend.
I smell his desperate aftershave from here. He's so well

hung, though, putting down the toilet seat. Pointing out
your oboe skills. Discussing you. Disgusting you—all
megaphoned, himself, one big notch down from his high
horse, yet oblivious to his falling. You still miss it? Then
deceive it. You no longer want to keep it? Fall in love.

OUR LAST BASTARD KISS

1.

In that moment between sleep and turning over,
I dance beneath an umbrella suspended
midair by a god's tangled kite string. No rain, but snow.

No sound, but white dissolving. Nothing
will forgive you for leaving. Every night I dig you up,
as if I can't get sicker, my framed photos throwing back

the TV light, where a studio audience
won't stop laughing. Perfect,
I go all insomniac again, a broken face-turned-woman-

turned-face, and yet I get away, cause a car crash,
then flip everyone the bird. I don't like dreams.
When I can't find myself, you show up

carrying a briefcase filled with seashells and a box
of white sand. We never visited the ocean. But we slept
beneath an umbrella once. Didn't we.

2.

I used to dress up as a dead
        girl back then, let you drag
my body through our high

school parking lot, my still-
        warm mouth fake-coughing
and wet with apple breath.

We sought a future that way,
        half alive most nights, cop
and robber. That was love,

I thought, because we hunted
        a cure, ripped the medicine
cabinet from the wall, found

my bobby pins, an old cheer-
        leading skirt, a corpse mask
with a sewn-in wig. I could live

in that disguise, touch you
        unclenched, not always afraid
of January nightmares,

where I woke up clutching
        cold in a fist. That was love,
I thought, because I wanted

to ruin all of you but couldn't
        find the blade in the pocket
of the costume I'd died in.

3.

You left me dirty, crouched down and dissecting
insect wings. After that, I wanted to feel you more than ever

as some pipe bomb stomach explosion, all shatter.
You could've had me raw, sucked

clean, my hands wrapped hot
around the moon, while all that time, my body

sang, whispering hailstorms into heartbeats. Understand—
you left me frenzied, holding

homemade soaps and a bleach-soaked rag, but the traffic still
moves past my new apartment. The neighborhood girl

who wears the grimy braids doesn't stop
pushing her wagon of stuffed monkeys, even though

the rain picks up, even though I yell for her
to go inside. You, my one experiment in slow-motion escape.

You, who always hated my small hometown.
Now I don't want anything but

Ohio. To be imprisoned, forgotten. To be that lost girl
pulling broken doll parts from the dumpster, concocting gods.

4.

And afterward, the moon stops looking like a moon
cartwheeling across the shadows
like an acrobat. It looks like a quarter soaked in lard
and taped to a chalkboard. According to that
conversion, a favorite song won't bring back the man
with the slingshot wit,
the bicep-washboard-bicep,
though the lyrics advise, in case of company, to wear
your soft-soled shoes. Considerate
to brush your teeth
before the pain. Considerate to tear up
his backyard weeds, to do it nude, by daylight,
by his breakfast nook, by outdoing
his every worst imagined unshaven horror story,
by god, by so opposite of silicone.
Then open the box
of tissues for a present. Or an aluminum replacement
earlobe for your tin-man lover. Whisper,
shake me. Thunder me so hard the car alarms.

THE INCIDENT WHEN MY DOG DIES AND/OR YOU LEAVE ME

I'm not unaware my dog's tail has stopped wagging,
that soon I will never see you again. Since I can't
hear what you most want to say, then tell me
with my talent what I can get away with.
You're admittedly an instant belly dancer
for anyone with a pretty brain. So save me.
At least meet me at the Slaughtered Lamb Pub,
so we can talk about the ceiling's splotched face,
or the infinite monkey theorem, or how it only
makes sense your favorite color is olive drab.
At some point in the night you'll turn on me,
but now I've got a voice and a winning dart team
named, "Tell Me I'm Lovely." Your fat black cat
loves me, too, which means I'm generally packing
in a way most others aren't packing—cats know.
When I sleep I dream I'm at the Kettle of Fish,
drinking and smoking so many menthols my tongue
tears into a doily, and for three whole minutes
I become a girl you think could save you. Even
your fat black cat came over to meow.

Let me show you something I once wrote for you:
I've slept alone I mean I've swept a lone cello
with a handkerchief to hear the timbre closest to
your voice. Now, you should notice the unoccupied
state of my hands, how my eyes scrape the floor
the minute you flaunt me a shoestring. I'm bored
with that talk, too, which is why I won't write
about the moon's whole gothic thing or how
the sun thinks she's too hot to touch. I want

that cello's moan, my dog back, or you,
and a neighbor's house. Let's live there, planting
daffodils. I've never touched a flower in my life,
give or take a body part or two. If I weren't this
confusing to others, you wouldn't sound so easy-
going next to me. If we weren't this close to the eve

of a burial, I might not worry that I can't hear
what you most want to say, though that whisper
in your throat just demolished a firefly.

IN A MINOR KEY, EVERYTHING RAINS

harder. That's not me poking fun at you. I like male flautists. I like wind
that screams in octaves, so blow me a kiss one last time for good this time.

Your tongue moves like a storm cloud, you wish, and lingers cold in the groove
of my cheekbone. I look at you staring at a reflection that hasn't occurred yet,

so desperate to commit to anything. Did I just say that? What I mean is, I can't
help but see the unfortunate importance in assuming your bones could feel.

In general. Get your mind out of the gutter. Repeat after me: *everything I touch
in bed I fail to shake like a percussion section.* I truly fucking hate you. All

this time you thought I was easy, but power lies in getting you to think it.
What I mean is, my heart is a plastic bastard disguised as a communication device.

I have a feeling I might turn living. Stop laughing, a girl died today you know,
or a girl you know died today. Which is it? To get you back on track:

your arms always felt like *stop*, you're a good candidate for the ten-yard dash,
and sometimes I lived a small percentage in the present, in case I loved you.

HE WATCHES DANCERS AT THE COUNTY FAIR

A girl rides by on an undersized tricycle. I scoff
at another girl in a cherry-colored tutu. He bites
into his fruit, his cake, whichever. Fireworks.
Is it night already? Costumed girls dance around,
leave the stage dragging scarves, their glittered
necks gleaming an invitation. When I watch him
watching them, the real noise begins. Somewhere
a child screams, a bass drum booms. I steal
my fake hand from his grip, open my fake mouth
but say nothing. Then the sky erupts into a dozen
dangling earrings that gradually disappear.

THE DAY BEFORE THE BREAKUP

I like the shapes the spider web creates,
yet that doesn't stop me from walking dead into it. That thud
the raindrops make on the air conditioner
sounds like someone heaving bullets
from the rooftop. Let's talk awhile as the moonlight eats

the quilt covering my face. My boyfriend always
puts his shoes under the table for me to kick and throw. Fasten
him to a clothesline, watch him dangle
with the rest of the laundry, drying off
that other girl in the breeze. If only I could avoid

my toes sticking out from the quilt my mother crocheted,
balls of yarn turned into joined circles. That other girl showed
her face again. I feel like a face gone
all cheekbones and frown, unimportant as the dead ant carried
by the living ant. I like packing

moving boxes, like to go back to bed once the sun
haunts the Earth. Watch the dumb fish
in the fishbowl. My heart gleans nothing. Boy, I'd rather
those shoes go in the closet, rather that girl go the way of nature
and follow the dandelion seeds.

HIV TEST RESULTS: FALSE POSITIVE

Everywhere I look, the trees spark fireworks. The car tires
explode and send the rims through windowpanes. My roommate drops
his clarinet and cuts his knee. All my plants turn back
to green again. I send my father off

to take his psychotropic meds, and he no longer crawls
inside the closet to destroy imaginary
rats that scratch
the walls while whispering

his name. And somewhere some fantastic
spider nest unleashes in a medicine cabinet. Flashback to that bathroom:
Uncle Curt still isn't dead
from AIDS and presses a needle

into his acne face. I'm six years old and take a break
from Tina Turner, watch him
squeeze the blood
and pus into a square of toilet paper,

not yet aware a man I love
will do the same one day. And I'll walk out. The blocks of sidewalk will sink
under my feet, greeting passersby by crumbling.
Then all my past

trespassers will discover me passed out
in a neighbor's outdoor tub, my shoeless feet, electric
blue toenails. My ex-boyfriend's girlfriend's margarita in one hand,
a cigarette in the other. Me engaged

in fantasies of me-as-leper, not sure about the weather or my Bible quotes.
My rash incurable, my urn
cleaned out. A broken crayon shooting
from the drain and coloring

a scene across my thigh: a woman
in some city gathers coins in paper cups, calls off her dogs when I float by
and hugs a half-peeled orange under her arm, while I tear up
a diagnosis with my teeth.

SLEEPING WITH SONNY GHOSTHORSE

He climbed on top of me and said, *My god
you're beautiful*, and so I stood to go,
           but tripped over the vacuum cleaner, smashed
my ass against the coffee table, rolled around
           and winced, became The Screamer,
the unleashed demon. Disclaimer: In the hours
           I've known him I've wanted to hock him,
hold him, diss him, dress him, drag him
           like a rake across the grass, and crack the iced
Ohio River with his bony frame, expose a little
           more than just his drug-addicted veins, marry
him off, die in his sleep, cry in his hat, nest
           in his shame, bore his father over crackers
and cheese, suck the breeze from his ponytail,
           kiss his kneecaps, or break them and carve
his dark heart out for the top of my
           Christmas tree, confiscate his pottery, speak
to him like a foreign film, abandoned, freak-
           showed, tornado-kind, entangled in his cartoon
suns, then let his hair fall back into a glass
           of rum, pretend he never said aloud and serious:
My conduit to god is eating strawberries in Paris.

HALF PERFUME, HALF SOMETHING ROTTEN

I should've stolen what you cultivated,
before frailty sprouted
from the seedling. The crops you planted in my teeth,
I should've eaten them. Instead,
my gums bled weeds
like a burial ground. My lips turned to buds.
You hosed them. I partway left,
and the cat missed me,
the rug curled up at the edges. Now here, in the home
I've grown inside your chin,
I sleep. Where else was I to live,
corn-toothed, a pistil for a tongue?
I rather like having taken
root in a face—the congregations
of cells slough off. I cling. Most of all, I want you
to feel what it's like
to be pricked, as my new thorn skates your skin,
hoeing the follicles. Would you believe what I found
there—all your past loves,
shied-up, crouching
down when I dig? And some music
pulsing slyly in the background.
They shimmied their petals like dresses when I came,
thinking I was you.
Inmates, they call us. But I enter
pores now. I breathe. Yes,
before, there were days when I traveled
from bed unhinged
to the ground, walked the sidewalk alone,
observed the gardens. So what does it mean
to have chosen captivity? Now for us, there is no last
touch. Sometimes I kiss
tree branches, and the flowers bow.

YOU ARE THE WASP NEST IN MY BROKEN RADIATOR

You are socks seeped through
with rainwater. You are the cobwebbed Christmas
lights I won't take down. I've known you forever,

if forever means walking backward
into traffic. All night long, I let you wreck
in dreams my body, my heart

the pinpricked thimble. You are bruises swelling
into prunes. You are the feral cat tiptoeing my fire
escape, your tongue rough lapping up

the window sweat. I follow you
around like a cop car scanning the streets
for a fugitive. But sometimes I settle

into your mix tapes, the music the background
to the ceiling fan twirling our shadows back to life.
There you kiss my neck so tenderly.

RELATIONSHIP REQUIEM
(ARRANGEMENT FOR KEYTAR)

My sister says: don't be mean to people
who don't understand you yet. That's logical
advice, and good, and no I'm not paying
for the new bedspread, even if it means losing.
Principles. Wasn't we good once? Wasn't we
committed? Listen, about last night: I curled up
with a new man, distant. Reasons, love:
the body, the body and its mean, sexy
keytar solo. A keytar strapped across the chest
lost you my love. My love? I fall for such
insignificant fools. Back to the beginning:
you make me feel like a tenor saxophone, all
copper-colored, chipped, some regretful wail.
Big deal, I seduced a new man. I was drunk,
panic-stricken, the stars winking, the stars
throwing up all over town, you in the role
of you-as-accomplice. Wasn't you a whisper?
Wasn't you vanished, little wallflower, up
the drummer's skirt? It's a mystery we woke
in bed together, the smell of sulfur, black holes
burnt into the bedspread, the bedspread still
warm all over our bankrupt bodies. Still,
I could try to be good, a playground in my
mouth, a soundtrack in my hair. Wasn't that
something I spoke to you in a dream?
Starting over: dear, I'm sorry I fucked
your best friend on top of his keytar, with you
as supporting actor, you as boom mic
operator, you as Mr. Miyagi, foreign, mono-
syllabic, asexual, pruning a bonsai tree

for seven hours straight. Then karate. Then
the severe ass kicking. Oh shush. All along
I'd meant to show you something that began
with losing: my body off limits, my body
passed around, my body burnt to asphalt under
the wretched trees. What a beauty I once was
in their light, before I learned to slink through
alleys, truck stops, the backwoods of your
hometown. Wasn't we committed? Wasn't we
in love—the drummer's skirt at the foot
of the bed, your best friend's strap-on
belly-synth glaring expensively on the clothesline?
You don't think we're sorry. Let's sleep awhile
longer under our last brief sky, the sun floating
like a charm against a white neck, all the fighting,
sex-starved clouds: such territorial bodies.

SYMPHONY FOR RED

All the red has been used up and buttoned
across the backs of butterflies and crowned
      upon the newly hatched cardinal's head, the red
unfurling feathers streaked with heat as bright
      as August sun and dark as cherry stems.
I've touched the broken checkmarks, zigged and zagged
      inside a tired eyeball—ant farms—red
and mean as fire, pulsing up like armies
      digging from a poison-threatened pupil,
the iris, optic nerve, and redder still
      the broken vessels near the nose's bridge.
They curl like forgotten threads dropped to the floor,
      a sewing kit gone mad with bleeding spools.
Even the scattered sky flags down the day
      with a red-tinged hat removed and flicked, a signal,
a shake of crimson here and there and *there*,
      beside the wide-mouthed cat greeting the dawn.
But gone an hour later. Instead—a blind-
      slat scar of yellow sunlight peeking through.
And gone—the vacuumed threads, the cardinal
      who unpacked the earth, its morning search for life—
a slithering meal. Like that. Just gone: a dash
      of rose across a cheek, a faded smack,
the starry flint of a cigarette alive
      on a lawn and left to scorch inside a hiss
of rain. Then back again—so soon—as rain
      begins the deeper stain of petals, bricks,
illuminates the stoplights, stop signs, red
      against the paint-chipped red that still, that *still*
exists even in dark. And then, a spark

of light, the clouds gathered like a thumping heart,
a spilling bowl of strawberries, then gone—
        like that—erotic sky turned gray and calm,
a vanished anger, quick to blur, dismissed,
        and absent still: your skin, your hands, your lips,
all gone—and weren't *they* red?

3. Pluck: To Take Away By Force

ON THE DEATH OF MY SISTER'S HUSBAND

I walk under the porch light, unprepared
for moths creeping the bulb, the buzz
eating my ears. I carry groceries
with one hand, apartment keys
with the other. The night flips on
its switch and keeps the moon all gorged,
the stars sketching a face across the sky,
then crackling with words
my sister unleashed into her phone
while I listen, in memory: she's broken,
of course, and begging for me
to reach through the network somehow,
the wires, until we can speak
her husband back to life, two voices
carrying in a morgue. I drop the keys
and prop the bag on my knee,
breathe a moment and try to think
of how black the moths look beating
against the glass, almost disappearing.
The keys glint like starlight on the ground,
the porch light winking back, the dark
gone dizzy, while the moon
continues fattening. I fall and knock
the bag over, my fingers catching
my apartment door. What waits there
but silence and the memory of a nighttime
just like this, where my sister made
a phone call, and I answered. I stand up
and place my key in the lock. Moths
keep breaking like my heart against the light.

PHONE CALL

When I got the phone call, I listened
to my sister's voice give
no hint, at first, that overnight,
like that, her life
had changed. I said *hello* and flipped through
a book on the nightstand, knowing
deep down, from all my missed
calls, that she was preparing
to tell me something
important. *How are you?* I asked,
trying to delay what I knew already
I didn't want to hear. And after
her silence, then, I sat straight up—I was still
in bed—my eyes blinking
awake, the automatic
coffee pot dripping into the quiet,
and I said it: *What's wrong, Heather?*
expecting for one singular moment the death
of our father, the sniffed
pills, the heroin finally ending
his life. But when she said
nothing, I demanded, this time, hearing
the pitch of her voice fill with the sound a brass
instrument might make breathing
a low note, barely
audible, into the crashing,
noisy universe. And she said it: *Joel killed himself
last night*, choking
on "killed," and when I said, *Oh
my god Heather*

oh my god, she understood, she told me
later, for the first time,
that her husband was never
coming back. The sun peeked through
the window blinds. It flashed across
the framed faces of his daughters, who I pictured,
for a second, on the swing set
behind their house, their father pushing them
higher each time they swung back to him, further
away each time, further away.

WHAT HAPPENED

What happened? I get the call. I spend a minute
staring into my window unit, my hair blown back
    and cold to the touch. *Like him?* I wonder,
grabbing my suitcase, grabbing my navy blue
    pantsuit and matching flats. *Do I need makeup?*
Heather will let me borrow hers. What happened?
    I imagine finding his body, how I'd laugh
like a fuckup detective on some TV show and joke,
    I guess he won't be needing these, lifting his keys
with my latexed finger toward a plastic bag.
    I'd place it next to his bank statement, the note
to his family written on the back: *I Am Sorry.*
    What a jerk, I'd think. *Who leaves three daughters
and a wife behind?* I snap back, tossing a book
    into my carry-on while waiting for the cab.
Delta, I say, but I'm not sure how it works
    when showing up at the airport unannounced
(like death) requesting a flight. *Departing now,*
    I whisper. *There's been an … accident*, although
I recognize the word's not right. What happened?
    At the service, no one breathes or blinks away
as I read the poem, "Hum": *the days are beautiful,*
    the days are beautiful. They stare into his photo
while Penelope, his youngest, keeps questioning
    the men. *Are you my daddy?* she asks. Chloe
and Sophia pretend to read their Dora books.
    What happened? Afterward, his family blames
my sister for everything. I hold her hand,
    the same hand I held when we hid under the bed
as children, the sitter smacking our baby brother

until his face turned blue. That's when we knew
the difference between a thing that we could stop
and what could stop us.

POSTMORTEM

I watched the beer drinkers
swig their cans while everyone warmed,
sweaty on the porch.

I heard the screen door wheeze
open to the living room,
where the lip
of a bottle cracked, threatening
the sheepskin.

An idiot rode the banister,
the sound of the vase he shattered
equaling his scream.

I blinked
with what behind my eyes felt
like a wet-nap.

(Funny for a minute
how a lampshade fascinated,
my fingers playing its hanging
threads like chimes.)

My mouth pinked on wine
and mistook each pill swallowed
for a smack.

I absorbed my distorted reflection
in the silver lock
where my sister ignored her
husband's ashes in a box.

Sometimes the room
airplaned into slits of light, like bones
heaved through a parking garage.

STORY

Just after he killed himself, I couldn't write
the word *pain*. I wrote *peonies*
and thought *ponies*, thought of ponies
and his daughters, and I sometimes felt

a breeze like a helicopter
hovering over dirt. When his daughters asked
for Daddy to hold them
toward the sky and spin, I translated

for a moment their laughter into hell.
I couldn't write the word *pain*,
but sometimes I wrote him back
into our story, digging up dirt to sturdy

for his girls a backyard tire swing that hung
from thick knots in rope.

NAMING GOODBYE

The first step: picture a field. Panting
heaps of grass.
Clouds: thumbprints
on the sky's face. A figure
in the field, waving
with the birds. No. Not the figure.
The field. Birds bleeding
into the distance. Picture the sun setting: a hidden
house, a crow's nest,
the battered sky. Its unraveling
belly. The figure, now
with a finger
in the moon's mouth. Try
again. Field:
a grass stain skidded
across a child's elbow. Yellowing
sky. Everything yawning. And the figure—
one cold hand reaching
up the sun's shirt.

NO RETURN ADDRESS

I lived a year once
in a country where no one knew me. It was a room
filled with paperweights and a screeching
in my head for days. I wrote a dead man
letters every night, and somehow
no one ever considered me
a maniac. Conversations showed up
as fist fights in slow motion, a silent film
montage of two bicycles colliding
over and over until finally I wrote
my own suicide notes, occasionally
with laughter, with a scraped knuckle, with a tree
in the background ruffling its bullshit,
and how could I not flip out
the light switch, angry
every night? At my worst,
I imagined living
inside a sewer, our favorite brunch spot perfuming
the streets above me where a waiter yelled
to a mother smacking her kid,
Be easy with that little boy.
When I said things like, *We desire so much
to please them, having been children ourselves
and hardly pleased,* my doctor begged me
to stop pushing everyone
I loved off a ledge. But I'd forgotten
who they were, whom I'd loved—the mouth-
pursing mom suspended over her Sunday *Times*
and coffee? The toddler endangering
the glassware with her drum? So, I wrote a dead man

letters every night, the streets below
my window, desperate
with ringtones, filling up and emptying
their getaway cars without me.

RUNNING OUT OF MEDICATION

I remember the man who told me once
not to bother him, how I imagined my hands
as talons on the hunt, how even then
I wanted to find the least
sharp part of myself
and touch him. When the meds run out
like that, everything burns. My mouth
turns hotter where a tongue
escaped. The sugar cubes meld to the bottom
of my coffee cup. I don't bother
with a coat. It drapes crooked
on the hanger as if inhabited
by a stranger, shrugging. On bad days,
insects move like marbles
tossed under the oven. I almost always end up
with a séance in my brain, little
mouths and their venom
destroying me in the supermarket, the library,
the bedroom. They whisper
Joel's name, consuming my whole mind
with the dead. The last pill falls
out of the bottle like a kid's tooth
from an envelope, but the nightmares terrorize,
watching a plane nosedive
while I hide in the bushes and try
to rescue no one. The pillow lies on the floor
like a blue body. I never wake lovely.

MENTAL HOSPITAL

At the back of my closet, a man's ashes were clumped
in a bag. I took a pill that lasted for days. I heard my own breathing,

watched a woman ride an elephant
in a tilted photo on the wall. The wind chopped

against the fan blades,
and I felt the whir like a machine

keeping me alive. I half-woke wanting.
My brain crawled me to the ground where the insects ticked,

where the lights blinking behind my eyes looked like a cup of coffee,
its pale flecks of milk. The people

reached to wake me, but I didn't know the people any more
than I knew the pill. They claimed to want to help me

know the real from the invisible: the white knobs
on the dresser from the bulbs of a bee's stinger. But every day I grew

coarse in the voice, swallowing
the pill's powder on the tongue, a fragment of frayed lint, a paper star.

DAYDREAM

I want to wake up one day, listen
with my ear against my bedroom floor to the water
bugs skittering, the cracks in the wood rousing

with me to the sun's sheen. Not like here,
in this coffee shop, dark, although the sun survives
enough to bleed through

the blinds, laying my shadow
black across the tile. Take me to the train station
where the people

seethe, where the tracks hum like a penny
placed against a windpipe. I miss
my sister's husband. Some days, he talks

to me when I drop my head against the pillow,
and I scream, pretend to grab his stupid face and say,
"No one knows, fucker, how to tell your girls

you killed yourself." Who cares
that he used to double fist
Budweiser cans with his daughter

on his lap? I secretly want to imitate that
cloud sticking out its tongue. But mostly, I love it
when the snowfall cuts its white across the fire

escape just outside the window, the sun falling
behind the powdery waves until it turns
back to drizzle, melting

the temporary pill shavings
to death again. No one knows how to save me
anymore. I was a lonely child. I grew up, breaking.

DEAR SOPHIA

Today I woke thinking my cat had died, balled up near
the heating vent. But it was a plastic bag of random trash,

a crumpled reminder bathing in the sun. I thought I'd feel
relief. I miss last year, my stagger from a Cincinnati bar,

you laughing at me, then yelling, "Steph, get up." Sorry
for buying the ornaments while drunk, crying, the bar lit

with a Christmas tree and names of all those AIDS victims
written across the paper decorations. I misspelled

my uncle's name. Did I tell you the dream
I had about our subway rats? They found a way out

of the underground alone. None of this makes sense.
Dear Sophia, I wake needing to tear my skin, to take it all

apart, to get it right. This time, I won't become surreal
although the moon's still evidence of some god's fingerprint.

The tree outside keeps dancing with a face intact. It's yours
or mine that dangles from the highest branch, like winter

apples, pale, no longer poisonous, not cold, not wanting
what's never close enough to have. Tonight, it's Christmas.

In Carolina, frozen ground, no snow. I hear it's white
all over Ohio, gathering a reflection. Of what? Listen.

I'm not drinking alone. There isn't a bell slicing through
your quiet dreams. I'm not reliving, no longer naming

everything a regret, a eulogy. What I can't help, I'm trying
to rebel against. I'm trying to undo the botched up

circumcision of the senses. Remember New York City,
how we fell, hitting our heads against a pole

in the subway car, those rats answering by hiding, like us,
in dark? We'd gotten good at blaming, at kissing one man

to wipe away another. Are you okay? I'd like a word,
a lie. Say, "home." Tell me the weather's fine.

WE REMEMBER YOU FOR NOW

Now when my heart beats, it sounds like
crunched leaves skittering, the revving up

of a broken-down Honda. I can't visit him
at a cemetery, or even the park. *Scatter*

my ashes there, he asked, and then injected
god knows how much, enough to warrant

a coroner call. *Hahaha*. Joke is Heather said
nope, stuffed and stored him in the back

of our mother's closet. He lives there now,
sucking up the radiator heat. Joel, damn,

man. Come back and lick the spilt fizz off
the Budweiser can again. No one here

is going anywhere if I have a say, and how
didn't I have a say with you? You plunged,

you syringed, each time needling—gentle,
I hope, as my grandmother crocheting

a winter hat for your oldest girl. I won't
for long torture myself for you, I thought,

biting into a string of candy hearts around
my neck, your kid insisting, eat it, the sick-

sweet sticky hands of a two-year-old with
a Dad resting inside a shoebox next to

a bowling ball. You did it. Congratulations.
I'm elated. I'm devastated. I'm a copycat

singing your songs to your girls to sleep.
Listen, creep: we remember you for now,

but now is a ragged dog, dragging its bum
leg along the buzzing halls of a new house.

HOW IT KEPT ON

My niece says that, when she grows up,
she wants to turn all the animals into rocks.
Three years old, already she pretends
to pull cicadas from her hair, hold them
on her tongue, and let them scream.
Someone told me once that children learn
to imitate our disarray. As a kid I used to
wonder what it would be like to go
from worn-in corduroys to all dolled up
in a dress, exposing nothing but a sliver
of clavicle. In Brooklyn now, at 29,
instead I watch the sun go down, pretend
the clouds explode into a flock of red
high heels descending. A man professed
on the train today that Jesus rides a UFO
to Earth and whispers to me while I sleep.
In that moment, I recalled the night
I watched my father use a spoon to crush
a pill, then sniff the powder off my history
book, how the world grew stranger then,
and afterward, how it kept on.

SO LONG

Someone else died again,
and when I heard, I felt
the green ocean
like a suffocating quilt
pulled over me. I had a father
once with a heroin
needle in his arm. So what am I
capable of? I'd rather flip
a book open than attend a party,
feel my numbed
fingertips in the cold and never
again hear my sister's voice
echo, "Joel killed himself
last night." Tell me how
someone leaves
and never comes back, how
the flying birds look
suddenly like his daughters'
black crayons thrown
through the air. If just one time
I could reach inside my mind,
unwrap it like those plastic
twist-offs sealing bread
from staleness, dance alone
in my room even when the room
houses ice. Joel killed himself,
and my nail polish
is chipped, my crosswalk
contaminated with taxis
like a speedway. I never visited

my father in prison, and I never
dance, but there's a man
who makes me laugh so hard
I spend some nights coming up
with plans to stay alive.

Winners of the Saturnalia Books Poetry Prize:

Also Available from saturnalia books:

Plucking the Stinger was printed using the fonts Kabel ITC and Adobe Garamond